A Touch of Christmas

by
Richard Exley

Tulsa, Oklahoma

Unless otherwise indicated, all Scripture quotations are taken from the *Holy Bible, New International Version* ®, NIV ®. Copyright © 1973, 1978, 1984 by International Bible Society. Used by permission of Zondervan Bible Publishers. All rights reserved.

A Touch of Christmas
ISBN 1-56292-251-3
Copyright © 1995 by Richard Exley
P.O. Box 54744
Tulsa, Oklahoma 74155

Published by Honor Books
P.O. Box 55388
Tulsa, Oklahoma 74155

Printed in the United States of America. All rights reserved under International Copyright Law. Contents and/or cover may not be reproduced in whole or in part in any form without the express written consent of the Publisher.

Presented to:

_____

On the Occasion of:

_____

Presented by:

_____

Date:

_____

Dedication

To Keith and Megan whose selfless love and unmitigated generosity are proof that the true Christmas spirit is alive and well.

Contents

Introduction

In this little book, I share with you a collage of thoughts and insights gathered across the years. They include: personal experiences — mine and others' — tidbits of wisdom, some Scripture and a lot of nostalgia, which have become, for the Exley household, the spirit of Christmas.

CHAPTER

1

*The Magic of
Christmas*

*"Go ahead, give
yourself to the
magic of Christmas."*

Chapter 1

The Magic of Christmas

Christmas – the very thought is nostalgic, invoking childhood memories of tinsel-covered trees, bright bows and colorfully wrapped packages. It brings to mind lighted nativity scenes, kids caroling in the cold, and hot chocolate in front of a roaring fire. It's love and laughter, fruitcake and pecan pie, childhood for a day.

Forget about life's pressing demands for a moment and embrace the Christmas spirit. Go ahead, give yourself to the magic of Christmas. Hear again the season's special sounds: carols coming from the big family radio, the running laughter of happy children, the murmur of conversation from aproned cooks in the kitchen.

Savor the smells: the aromatic scent of pine from the tree in the middle of the high-ceilinged living room (no artificial trees when you were a child); the tart-sweet odor of hot apple cider steaming on the stove;

the rich aroma of pies cooling on the counter; the tantalizing smell of holiday meals in the making.

Replay the scenes on the screen of your mind. See again: overshoes in the corner of the kitchen, sitting in a puddle of melted snow; kids, cheeks flushed from the cold, toasting their toes over the wheezing floor furnace; a happy family playing table games while outside huge snowflakes blanket the world in winter white.

Experience again the full range of emotions these memories invoke. Let them play a nostalgic melody on the strings of your heart. Remember the warmth of a special friendship, the comfort of kindness, the closeness of family. Think about the Christ child in Bethlehem's manger and the nearness of God.

Blink back the tears, if need be, and swallow past the fist-size lump in your throat, but don't quench the memories. They are a part of your history, part of the web of experience which God has woven into the tapestry of your personhood.

Examine it. Celebrate it! Share it with your spouse, your children. No gift you can give will be more lasting or more deeply appreciated. Long after the toys have been discarded, and the clothes outgrown, your loved ones will remember and cherish your memories of Christmases past.

Where is God in all of this?

Why, just where He has always been – in the thick of it! For God is at the heart of Christmas, manifesting Himself in life's ordinariness:

A baby, born in a dung-infested sheep shed, to peasant parents.

Shepherds stumbling all over themselves in their excitement to answer the angelic summons.

An old man, a priest, seeing his dreams – and the dreams of all the ages – fulfilled in this obviously ordinary-looking child.

Even now God is revealing Himself as He always has – through the birth of a child, the joy of common men, or in the toothless musing of an old priest.

Remember, for those who pause to listen the angels still sing, "Glory to God in the highest, and on earth peace, good will toward men."[1]

---

[1] Luke 2:14 KJV.

THE TRUE CHRISTMAS SPIRIT

Lord,
Deliver us from the spirit of consumerism,
from shopping lists,
full color catalogs,
and credit card purchases
which haunt us for the rest of the year.
Deliver us from empty cheer and seasons greetings
     born of obligation,
            sent without meaning.
Deliver us from the whirl of social events
which supposedly honor Jesus' birth
but in reality are nothing more
than another desperate attempt
to coax some joy and meaning
into a life filled to the brim with busyness.
Surely Christmas is supposed to be more than this;
more than another round in our bumper car existence:
     "How are you doing?"
     Bump, bump.

"Great party isn't it?"
Bump, bump, bump...

Grant us the true Christmas spirit, Lord.
The generosity of heart,
the self-forgetfulness,
the love which caused You to wrap Yourself
in the garments of our humanity
and live among us for a time.

Grant us the true Christmas spirit, Lord.
The genuine joy of authentic celebration —
angels singing,
shepherds stumbling through the dark
in search of the Savior,
Elizabeth's song, Simeon's prophecy,
Anna's exclamation of praise!

Grant us the true Christmas spirit, Lord.
Hymns of faith sang from the heart,

true worship,
candlelight communion,
prayer more real than words.
The simple pleasure of family and friends,
the excitement of children,
adult conversation laced with memories,
childhood remembered and relived for a day.
Grant us the true Christmas spirit, Lord.

Amen.

CHAPTER

2

A Homemade
Christmas

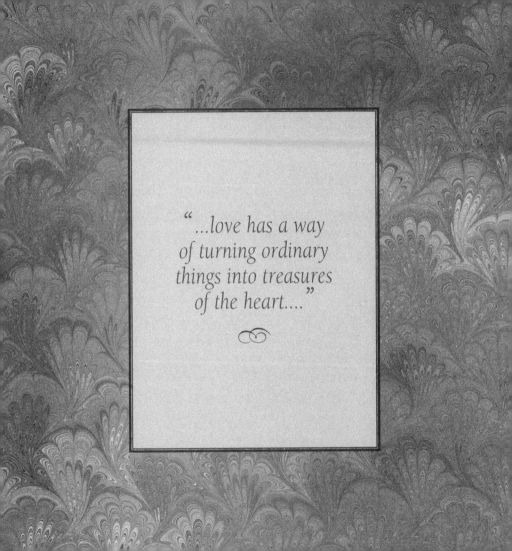

"*...love has a way
of turning ordinary
things into treasures
of the heart....*"

Chapter 2

A Homemade Christmas

As Christmas approaches, I find myself reminiscing, reliving the joys of Christmases past. Several memories come to mind – family gatherings, candlelight Christmas Eve services and the excitement of a long-awaited gift. Special though such memories are, tonight my mind is drawn to something else, to the bittersweet poignancy of a Christmas more than two decades ago.

Thinking about it now, it all comes rushing back, and it's nearly as real as it was then. Brenda and I are just "kids" – she is twenty, and I am a year older – serving our first church. It's a small fellowship, numbering less than thirty members, located in the farming community of Holly, Colorado, in the southeast corner of the state. It has been a lean year, and financially things are tight for us. If the truth be known, we are flat broke, and there isn't a way in the world we can afford gifts for those we love.

As I stand before the window in my small study, brooding over our unhappy plight, I recall a scene from Truman Capote's little book, *A Christmas Memory*. Seven-year-old Buddy and his distant cousin, a white-haired woman of sixty-something with whom he lives, are making Christmas gifts. "Tie-dye scarves for the ladies, for the men a homebrewed lemon and licorice and aspirin syrup to be taken 'at the first Symptoms of a Cold and after Hunting.'"[1]

For each other they are building kites, like last year and the year before that. Kites are not their first choice, but their creativity is severely crimped by their poverty. If money were no object, she would buy him a bicycle, and he would get her a pearl-handled knife, a radio and a whole pound of chocolate-covered cherries.

Suddenly she looks up, her bright eyes gleaming, and says with a frightful intensity, "'It's bad enough in life to do without something *you* want; but confound it, what gets my goat is not being able to give somebody something you want *them* to have. Only one of these day I will, Buddy. Locate you a bike. Don't ask how. Steal it maybe.'"[2]

That same feeling, or its close kin, now churns in my chest. A flannel nightgown is what I want to buy Brenda and a fuzzy housecoat to

---

[1] Truman Capote, *A Christmas Memory* (New York: Random House, Inc., 1956), p. 36.
[2] *Ibid.*, p. 37.

keep her warm against the winter cold, which has a way of finding every crack in this old parsonage. Earlier, when we still had hopes of a Christmas windfall, she mentioned how nice it would be to have one.

Of late she has concerned herself with other things, like Christmas decorations which we already have from last year. Beneath her determined gaiety, though, I sense her disappointment. Not about the nightgown, she can do without that. What troubles her is not being able to purchase gifts for those she loves.

Brenda is a champion gift-giver, and no one enjoys it more. She has been known to spend hours, days even, searching for the perfect gift. Unfortunately, with Christmas less than a week away, it is becoming readily obvious that there will be no shopping spree for her this year, no opportunity to search for that perfect gift.

We try to encourage each other. She reminds me that we are blessed with loving families and caring friends. Agreeing, I add that no one has a right to complain who has a roof over his head and food enough to eat. Still, in spite of our brave assurances, self-pity seeps into our spirits.

Brenda does what she can to make the holidays special. She decorates the house and bakes Christmas goodies to the accompaniment of carols emanating from the clock-radio which sits on the kitchen counter. I try to get in the holiday spirit, too; but in truth, it all seems futile to me. Even the tinsel-covered tree, standing before the window in the living room, looks somehow forlorn without any Christmas packages beneath its evergreen bows. At least it seems so to me.

More and more I find myself succumbing to lengthy periods of self-pity. I hate it, but I seem powerless to do anything about it. Moping around the house, I nearly drive Brenda to despair.

Finally, she takes matters into her own hands and on a bright sunlit morning three days before Christmas she announces, "We may not be able to afford to buy gifts, but we can make them."

Though I attempt to talk her out of such madness, citing my artistic ineptitude, there is no reasoning with her. Her mind is made up, and in a few minutes we are bundled up and in the car.

As I drive, hunched behind the wheel like a youthful Scrooge, she ignores me and with childlike excitement describes the arrangement she intends to make for her parents from spray-painted wildflowers and driftwood.

"And what," I ask sullenly, trying to bait her into an argument, "am I supposed to make my folks?"

Refusing to take the bait, she continues her Christmas monologue with unabashed enthusiasm. By the time we reach the river bottom south of town, I am beginning to warm up to the idea myself. Maybe I'll make my folks a TV lamp. If I use parts salvaged from a discarded lamp left by a previous pastor, it will cost almost nothing.

Parking the car, we step into a dazzling world of winter beauty. December frost has coated every branch and thistle with a brilliance that glitters and dances against the blue of the sky. Even the unsightly strands of rusting barb wire have been transformed into a thing of beauty.

Frost-coated yellow grass crunches beneath our feet as we set out in search of raw materials from which to create a Christmas like none we have ever had before. Brenda heads downriver, while I turn upstream in search of the perfect piece of driftwood. We split up, not because we are angry, at least not anymore, but because we can cover more ground this way. From time to time we call to each other, and clouds of vapor accompany our shouted words.

After a couple of hours we return to the car to sort our booty. Brenda has gathered spiky Russian thistles, milkweed pods and an assortment of dried flowers which we can't identify. My contribution is a collection of driftwood.

Once our materials are safely packed away, she extracts a thermos of hot chocolate from the back seat. As we munch on Christmas cookies, the bright December sun washes the last of the frost from the river bottom, leaving it a dull brown. It does nothing, however, to dampen our rejuvenated spirits. As we drive home, I find myself thinking that it is finally starting to feel like Christmas.

Back at the parsonage, we set up shop on the kitchen table. Using a variety of supplies left over from her crafts, Brenda creates a dried-flower arrangement of rustic beauty. After cannibalizing the discarded lamp from the cellar, I use the salvaged parts and a driftwood stump to make my folks a TV lamp, which sits in their bedroom still.

Somehow we manage to make it home for Christmas, and in the company of family and friends our poverty is soon forgotten. It returns momentarily when it is time to open the gifts, and we wait with fearful pride for our parents to make over our handiwork. They do not disappoint us. In truth, they seem to cherish these homemade gifts above the more expensive store-bought ones of later years.

More than a quarter-century has passed since that fateful Christmas, and we have had many opportunities to exchange gifts. On occasion they have been rather extravagant, at least by our modest standards. Still, when I think of the joy of giving, it is to that homemade Christmas that my thoughts return. Perhaps it's because love has a way of turning ordinary things into treasures of the heart, and that's what Christmas is all about.

Lord,
Christmas is just days away
and once gain I am eaten up
with my annual insecurities.
Materialism and self-doubt
dominate my thoughts.
Everyday,
or so it seems,
we receive another full color catalog.
Their glamorous offerings
not only tempt me to lust after things
I do not need and cannot afford,
but they also raise doubts
about my ability
to provide for those I love.
I mean,
if I don't shower my family
with the latest fashions
and electronic gear,
then maybe I'm not really
a loving husband or a generous parent.
On another level,
all this glitz and holiday hype
stimulates my personal insecurities.

I'm too short,
     too heavy,
          too old.
As a result I'm tempted
to go on a spending spree
in a misguided attempt
to make myself acceptable,
to become one of the "beautiful people."

Help me Lord.
Remind me again
that the true message of Christmas
affirms my worth apart from what I have,
     or what I do.
Help me to remember
that You became the "Son of man,"
that we might become the sons of God.
Now that's the real meaning of Christmas
and it proves I am a person of eternal value
even if I can't afford the latest fashions
     or electronic gear.

Amen.

CHAPTER

CHAPTER

3

Sacramental Moments

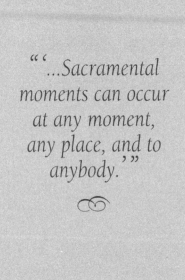

" '...Sacramental
moments can occur
at any moment,
any place, and to
anybody.' "

Chapter 3

Sacramental Moments

In the truest sense, Christmas is not just a holiday, it's a happening. It's something that happens to you, something you haven't earned and definitely don't deserve. It's something God does, a gift of grace, a sacramental moment.

That's what it was for the shepherds that first Christmas so long ago. After a hard day of tending sheep, they are sitting around the fire swapping stories — telling lies most likely, as men are wont to do when they talk about themselves. And they are doing some other things too, that we dare not mention in polite company.

Suddenly, the night is ablaze and they find themselves immersed in the glory of the Lord, or as Luke puts it, "...the glory of the Lord shone around them...."[1] And out of the glory an angel appears with a startling

---

[1]Luke 2:9.

announcement: "...'I bring you good news of great joy....Today in the town of David a Savior has been born to you; he is Christ the Lord. This will be a sign to you: You will find a baby wrapped in cloths and lying in a manger.'"[2]

"Suddenly a great company of the heavenly host appeared with the angel, praising God and saying, 'Glory to God in the highest, and on earth peace to men on whom his favor rests.'"[3]

It's important, I think, to note that there is nothing at all in this account to suggest that anything religious was going on around that campfire. Nor is there anything in the Scriptures to lead us to believe that the shepherds did anything to precipitate that angelic announcement. In truth, there is not a shred of evidence to indicate that they were in any way special; nothing to suggest that there was anything in their spirit, or nature, or lifestyle that predisposed them to receive this angelic announcement.

Which, I believe, is precisely why God chose them. In first-century Judea, shepherds were mostly considered outcasts. Respectable people simply didn't socialize with them. They were the lowest cast in the

---

[2]Luke 2:10-12.
[3]Luke 2:13,14.

social system, and to our way of thinking, the least likely to receive a supernatural visitation.

This, I believe, is the message of Christmas. It begs us to wake up and realize that the holy doesn't just happen to religious people in the house of God, but to undeserving people the world over, be it lepers or lunatics, shepherds or Samaritans, or even women taken in adultery.

"...Sacramental moments," as Frederick Buechner says, "can occur at any moment, any place, and to anybody. Watching something get born, making love, a high school graduation, somebody coming to see you when you're sick, a meal with people you love, looking into a stranger's eyes and finding out he's not a stranger. If we weren't blind as bats, we might see that life itself is sacramental."[4]

Sometimes God comes to us, as He did to the shepherds, through a mystical experience, a vision if you please. More often than not, though, He reveals Himself in more mundane ways — like "...a baby wrapped in cloths and lying in a manger."[5] He may come as words of encouragement spoken by a friend in the dark hour of unspeakable sorrow, or in a child's smile, or even in the words of a sermon.

---

[4]Frederick Buechner, *Wishful Thinking*, quoted in *Disciplines for the Inner Life* by Bob Benson and Michael W. Benson (Waco: Word Books, 1985), p. 201.

[5]Luke 2:12.

Christmas invites us to pause in the mad rush of living and examine our lives. As we do, more often than not, we belatedly realize that God is with us, that He has been there all the time, even when we paid Him no mind, even when we were sure He was nowhere to be found.

For instance, when I was sixteen I went swimming in the South Platte river on a hot August afternoon with a pretty girl who would later become my wife. Carelessly, we splashed in the river, oblivious to the sun's deadly rays. Later that evening, I rubbed Noxzema Skin Cream on her sunburned shoulders. That, I think, is when I discovered I was in love, and to this day Noxzema Skin Cream smells like love to me.

Only now, these many years later, do I realize that the source of my joy that sunlit afternoon was not young love, but God. He was the One Who brought us together, Who made our running laughter a kind of holy music, Who destined that we would one day marry and give birth to a child of our own.

Now, before you decide I have lost my mind or committed a sacrilege, take a minute and remember how often God revealed Himself to ordinary people in the most mundane ways. The best known, of course, is the Incarnation — God incognito — or as John says, "The Word became flesh and made his dwelling among us...."[6]

---

[6]John 1:14.

Most of the world missed that sacramental moment because it came wrapped in such provincial trappings. As far as the busy innkeeper was concerned, Jesus was just another baby. To His childhood friends and neighbors in Nazareth, He was the carpenter, Mary's son, nothing more.[7] Even Mary Magdalene succumbed to the myth, supposing Him to be the gardener.[8]

The two despairing disciples on the road to Emmaus mistook Him for a stranger. Only later, after He departed from them, did they realize who He was and exclaim, "...'Were not our hearts burning within us while he talked with us on the road...?'"[9]

To Peter and his fishing buddies, He was just a beachcomber squatting beside a breakfast fire in the early morning mist. Only later, after He called them to breakfast, did they recognize Him as the Lord.[10]

What am I trying to say? What is Christmas trying to say to us? Just this: "Listen to your life. See it for the fathomless mystery it is. In the boredom and pain of it no less than in the excitement and gladness.

---

[7] Mark 6:3.

[8] John 20:15.

[9] Luke 24:32.

[10] John 21:4-14.

Touch, taste, smell your way to the holy and hidden heart of it because in the last analysis all moments are key moments, and life itself is grace."[11]

In his little book, *Now and Then*, Frederick Buechner puts it so clearly: "By examining as closely and candidly as I could the life that had come to seem to me in many ways a kind of trap or dead-end street, I discovered that it really wasn't that at all. I discovered that if you really pay attention to it, even such a limited and limiting life...opens up onto extraordinary vistas. Taking your children to school and kissing your wife good-bye, eating lunch with a friend, trying to do a decent day's work, hearing the rain patter against the window. There is not an event so commonplace but that God is present within it, always hidden, always leaving you room to recognize him, but all the more fascinatingly because of that, all the more compellingly and hauntingly."[12]

Now that's the real meaning of Christmas, isn't it? Immanuel, God with us!

---

[11]Frederick Buechner, *Wishful Thinking*, quoted in *Disciplines for the Inner Life* by Bob Benson and Michael W. Benson, p. 120.

[12]Frederick Buechner, *Now and Then*, quoted in *Disciplines for the Inner Life* by Bob Benson and Michael W. Benson, p. 120.

Lord,
When You became one of us
You did not come as a man,
but as a child.
You,
      the eternal Word,
           the infinite God,
became a microscopic zygote
clinging to the wall of Mary's womb.
Through the miracle
and the mystery of life
You became a tiny fetus,
      living for a few short months
      in the warmth and safety
      of Your mother's body.
Then You were born
and the mystery of Your life in the womb
was revealed for all the world to see.

From a babe in Mary's arms
You grew into a toddler,
      a child.

By this, the act of incarnation,
>   You have forever given,
>   to every child,
>   a special dignity and worth.
You have made them
a living treasure,
>   a holy treasure.
Each and every child
>   is eternally precious.

Help us I pray,
as both parents and friends,
to be faithful stewards to these little ones.
May we nurture them
>   with Your unconditional love.
May we discipline them
>   with Your unerring faithfulness.
And may we train them
>   in Your eternal truth,
especially at Christmas time.
In Jesus name we pray.

Amen.

CHAPTER

4

Christmas
Traditions

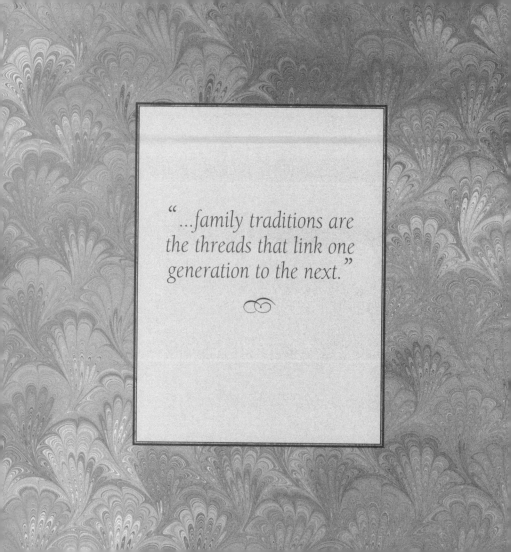

"*...family traditions are the threads that link one generation to the next.*"

Chapter 4

Christmas Traditions

Memorable Christmases don't just happen. They have to be created, and at our house Brenda is the creator of Christmas, after God that is. Each year there comes a morning, shortly after Thanksgiving, when she decides it is time to make another Christmas. After I leave for the office and Leah has gone to school, Brenda goes into the garage and locates the box containing the flocked Christmas tree. With a herculean effort she drags it into the house where she assembles the tree in preparation for decorating, all the while listening to the Carpenter's Christmas album.

Once the tree is assembled, she makes repeated trips to the attic, returning each time with an armload of dusty boxes containing decorations for the tree. With an artist's eye, she blends things both old and new, creating a seasonal masterpiece that is the envy of all our friends.

Next, she turns her attention to the mantle above the fireplace. Using Christmas candles, kerosine lamps and a picturesque Christmas story book, she creates a scene reminiscent of the Christmases she spent as a child on her grandparents' farm in South Texas. There, the traditions of a German Christmas were reenacted without fail.

As the day draws to a close, she places a beautiful wreath on the front door, then fastens yards and yards of garland, festooned with red and green, on the staircase in the entry before hanging mistletoe in every doorway. Finally, she assembles the weihnachtz pyramide from Aachen, Germany, a gift from our dear friends the Merrells. With its candles and creche, it becomes the focal point of all the decorations, for were it not for our Lord's birth in Bethlehem we would have nothing to celebrate.

In the days immediately preceding Christmas, she is a dynamo of ceaseless activity. In addition to spending hours, whole days really, haunting the shopping malls in search of just the right gift for everyone on her list, she also prepares a host of traditional Christmas goodies. Wearing a holiday apron, she labors in the kitchen, turning out homemade fudge, platters of divinity, kalachie and an assortment of pies, including pecan, peanut butter and a dutch apple that is my favorite.

Stepping into our house during December is like entering another world. Christmas music plays constantly. A teapot of apple cider simmers on the stove, filling the kitchen with the fragrance of apples and cinnamon. Candles and kerosine lamps become our primary source of light, casting a warm yellow glow that transports us back to an earlier, simpler time when families gathered around the fireplace or wood stove and spent the long winter evenings together. For a time each evening we are able to escape from the busy world and experience again the simple joy of family and friends.

On Christmas Eve we dress in our holiday best and join our church family for a special time of worship and communion. Returning home, we share a meal before gathering around the fireplace for our annual reading of *A Christmas Memory* by Truman Capote. Finally, we open our gifts.

It's hard work creating a Christmas like that, dragging boxes in and putting up lights and decorations. Still harder work taking the same decorations down and dragging the boxes back out. That's why you really have to have a heart for Christmas in order to create one. Some people are born with a gift for it, but most of us learn from those who first made Christmas for us.

Brenda was "tutored" by her mother, Hildegarde, who faithfully made Christmas special at the Wallace house. As a child growing up, she remembers big Christmas trees, gaily wrapped packages and a richly decorated living room. Hildegarde continued this tradition as long as the girls brought their families home for Christmas.

A few years ago we were spending Thanksgiving with the Wallaces at their retirement home in East Texas when Brenda asked, "Mom, when are you going to put up your Christmas decorations?"

Quick as a flash, Hildegarde said, "I'm not decorating for Christmas this year."

"What?" Brenda asked in disbelief. "You always decorate for Christmas."

"Not any more," Hildegarde explained. "It's too much trouble when your Daddy and I are the only ones who will be here. You're having Christmas in Tulsa with Leah. Scott's having Christmas in Nacogdoches, and Linda will be staying in Houston for the holidays." And then we knew, maybe what we should have known all along. Hildegarde really didn't enjoy putting up the Christmas tree or decorating the house. What she enjoyed was the pleasure her children and grandchildren derived from her labor of love. So it is, I suspect, with most all of you who labor faithfully year after year to make Christmas special for those you love.

We are indebted to you, for you are the custodians of our family traditions, the keepers of those holiday rituals that enhance the richness of the season. As such, you provide an invaluable service, for family traditions are the threads that link one generation to the next.

Lord,
You are the eternal architect of Christmas,
the creator of this,
>the most wonderful of all seasons.

Though we have exploited it,
>prostituted it for profit,
>>and turned it into a materialistic orgy,

still it remains the holiest of all days.
At least for one day each year
the world pauses in its mad busyness
and our hearts turn toward home.
With nostalgic tenderness
we recall the joys of Christmases past
while contemplating the mysteries
of God and family.
Dim memories of our childhood faith
tug at our hearts
and we realize anew
that we are truly spiritual beings,
>men and women made in the image of God.

Within our hearts hope burns eternal

and on Christmas day we believe all things are possible:
> Sins can be forgiven,
>> broken relationships can be restored,
>>> hurts can be healed,
>>>> and best of all
>>>>> God is with us!

Thank you Lord,
for creating Christmas
and may we never forget
that You are the one
who puts Christmas into our hearts
and calls us unto Yourself.

Amen.

CHAPTER

5

*A Country
Christmas*

"*Nothing* can take the place of a three-generation holiday when it comes to giving a child a sense of family and a place to belong."

Chapter 5

A Country Christmas

Another Christmas has come and gone. Your husband's family has taken their leave, and the house is finally quiet after nearly a week of wall-to-wall people. As you climb the stairs toward your daughter's room, you breathe a prayer of thanksgiving. It's been a wonderful holiday season, howbeit a tiring one.

Tucking your daughter into bed, you make yourself comfortable beside her and settle down for your bedtime chat. Her eyes sparkle with happiness as she regales you with stories about her cousins. Finally, she grows quiet and after a moment she asks, "Mommy, did you ever spend Christmas with your cousins?"

Her question carries you back to your own childhood, and a host of memories wash over you. You remember the farm at Cheapside and the good times you had. In the summer you sunbathed with your sister while lying on a raft in the tank. Often you were joined by your cousin Carla Dawn, and the three of you played hide 'n seek in the corn field and chased each other through the peach orchard. In the evenings you would sit on the top rail of the corral and watch Nannie and Papo milk the cows. Then it was into the house for supper and a bath before bedtime.

A soft smile plays across your face as you remember the simple happiness of those carefree days. Your daughter tugs at your sleeve, pulling you back to the present. When you look at her she asks, "Well, did you, Mommy, did you?"

Nodding a reply, you ask, "Would you like to hear about it?"

Her happy smile is all the answer you need, and taking a deep breath you begin...

"Times were different when I was a girl, especially on the farm where Nannie and Papo lived. There was no indoor toilet, just an outhouse."

She wrinkles up her nose and says, "Yuck!"

You smile and continue, "To get to the outhouse we had to go through the chicken pen, and there was one mean old rooster who hated me. Every time I went to the outhouse, he would chase me. Any time I had to go to the bathroom, I would beg for one of the adults to go with me. They just scoffed at my fears and said, 'Don't be afraid. He won't hurt you.'

"I tried to be brave, but it wasn't long until that rooster cornered me against the side of the outhouse. He clawed my face and arms as I stood there screaming with pain and fear. To this day I can't remember how I got away — most likely Nannie or Papo rescued me — but I'll never forget what happened to that rooster. Papo killed him, and we ate him for Sunday dinner."

Your daughter looks at you skeptically, then asks, "Did that really happen?"

"You better believe it happened."

She's still skeptical, but now she presses you to tell her about Christmas on the farm.

You pause to collect your thoughts, then you begin: "It's Christmas Eve, and as daylight fades a norther plunges the temperature toward freezing. Papo is worried about the cattle, but the threatening weather only adds to the holiday excitement as far as us girls are concerned. There's three of us — my sister Linda, our cousin Carla Dawn, and me.

"'Is it going to snow, Papo?' we ask with unmitigated excitement, 'Is it going to snow?'

"'I certainly hope not,' he says grumpily as he heads into the kitchen to catch the weather report on the radio.

"His gruffness does not faze us. Already the day has exceeded our wildest expectations – Papo surprised us with a trip to Cheapside where he bought us ice cream in a paper cup and soda pop at the country store – and once we finish our baths we'll eat supper and then play until bedtime.

"The bath tub is huge and made of cast iron with claw-like feet that hold it off the floor. There is no hot water heater, so Nannie heats the water on the kitchen stove and then fills the tub nearly to the brim. Once this is done, all three of us girls crawl in.

"Suddenly, Aunt Erma's broad frame fills the doorway. 'Use lots of soap,' she says, 'and don't forget to wash under your arms.'

"We nod obediently, but once the door closes behind her we burst into giggles. In an instant I am out of the tub and searching for Papo's shaving brush and mug. Once I locate it, I get a can of Daddy's shaving cream and a small comb. Back in the bath tub, I cover Linda's face with shaving cream and shave her with the comb. Not to be outdone, Carla Dawn gets two handfuls of shaving cream and makes herself some 'boobs.' Linda and I laugh hysterically when they begin to droop, and then we try it ourselves with the same dire results.

"The window above the bath tub has steamed over, and Linda writes her name in the dampness. Carla Dawn and I follow suit and then play tic-tac-toe on the wet pane. Aunt Erma calls from the kitchen, telling us that supper is on the table. Her gruff German abruptness leaves no room for dallying around, so we frantically scrub ourselves and leap from the tub, dripping water all over the floor.

"In a matter of minutes, we are dressed and at the table. The women have prepared a feast: just everything you can imagine, from pan-fried chicken and home-canned corn to homemade bread right out of the oven with lots and lots of butter. For dessert there's Nannie's famous coffee cake. The adults gorge themselves, but we hardly touch a thing. It's Christmas Eve, and we are too excited to eat.

"As soon as we can, we escape to Nannie and Papo's bedroom where we play Peter Pan. Leaping from bed to bed, we pretend to fly. Suddenly, there is a banging on the living room window, and our hearts freeze with fear. Creeping to the bedroom door, we watch as Papo opens the window to see what's going on.

"'Why, it's Santa Claus,' he says. Turning to us, he calls, 'Look here, girls, it's Santa Claus. Come tell him what you want for Christmas.'

"Cautiously, we emerge from the bedroom, unable to believe our eyes. I'm scared out of my mind and cannot be persuaded to go near the window. Fearlessly, Linda and Carla Dawn march right up to Santa. After presenting their Christmas lists, they precede to kiss him on the cheek and burst into giggles when his whiskers tickle their faces.

"Only later did we learn that it wasn't really Santa Claus at all, but just our neighbor Mr. Staley dressed in a Santa costume.

"Finally, it is time for bed, and mother makes a pallet on the floor, in front of the Christmas tree, out of homemade quilts. After tucking us three girls in, she prays with us and shuts out the lights. We pretend to sleep until the house grows quiet, then we whisper and giggle in the dark.

"After a while, Carla Dawn and I get hungry, so we tiptoe to the kitchen where we find a head of lettuce. Cutting it in half, we sprinkle it with salt and run back to our bed. Once we are safely ensconced under the covers, we make like rabbits and crunch our booty as loudly as possible. Linda hates lettuce, and our crunching drives her nearly mad, which we think is great fun.

"Awaking early on Christmas morning, we huddle in the warmth beneath the quilts, while the big stove in the corner of the living room slowly drives the chill from the old farmhouse. Finally, we venture forth and run barefoot across the living room to stand shivering around the stove. Mother warms our clothes before the fire and then she helps us dress.

"At long last it is time to open our presents, and we gather around the Christmas tree almost out of our minds with excitement. Surely we received more than one present, but all I can remember are the bride dolls. There was one for each of us. Mine had a porcelain face, real hair and eyelashes. She was dressed in the most gorgeous bride's dress and veil. I don't believe I've ever seen a more beautiful doll, not even to this day.

"Mother and Aunt Erma spent hours and hours making those dresses. Every stitch was a work of art. Without question, it is the most memorable gift I received as a child, and to this day I cherish it.

"The rest of the day follows a familiar routine with Christmas dinner being a highlight. Everything Nannie serves is raised right there on the farm, except for the strawberry ice cream, of course. It's a gorgeous meal: a golden brown turkey stuffed with cornbread dressing, giblet gravy, candied sweet potatoes with marshmallows on top, Irish potatoes mashed, home-canned corn, pickled beets, dill pickles, fruit salad and homemade hot rolls with lots of butter and honey which had turned to sugar. For dessert there is a homemade angel food cake with seven-minute icing.

"Once dinner is finished, we girls retreat into the bedroom to rehearse our annual performance. Sometimes we quote poems, but more often than not we sing songs that we have learned in Sunday school. As we grow older, we play musical instruments or act out the Christmas story. Finally, everyone gathers in the bedroom around Nannie's pump organ, and we sing carols and the great hymns of the church."

Glancing down, you discover that your daughter has fallen asleep. For a moment you are disappointed, then you realize that your reminiscing was as much for yourself as it was for her anyway. It's good to remind ourselves, you decide, how valuable family traditions are. Nothing can take the place of a three-generation holiday when it comes to giving a child a sense of family and a place to belong.

Lord,
Thank you for the gift of family —
    parents and grandparents,
        brothers and sisters,
            aunts and uncles,
                cousins and other kin.
From them we get our identity,
    our personhood.
They give us a sense of history
    and a place to belong.
In times of crisis they provide a safe haven
    and when sorrow comes they are our strength,
        a source of comfort in the dark hour
            of unspeakable loss.
In a world beset with change
cultural evolution threatens the traditional family,
still it remains the best connection
we have with our personal past.
In truth, family traditions are the threads
    which link one generation to the next.
They provide a kind of ritual

which makes holidays not only special
but somehow sacred as well.
Remind us, Lord,
that the first Christmas was a family event.
Teach us to make all of our Christmases
family celebrations where we remember,
not only Mary and Joseph
and Your special birth,
but our own family us well.
In Your holy name we pray.
Amen.

CHAPTER

6

Special Gifts

" *...their joy cannot compare with ours for we experience the special joy of helping make a dream come true for someone we love.* "

Chapter 6

Special Gifts

*F*ollowing the Christmas Eve Communion service, we all gather in the living room, in front of the fireplace, to exchange gifts. Mom reaches over and takes Dad's hand, and I am moved by the tenderness that passes between them. He looks at her and smiles; and I breath a prayer of thanksgiving, realizing again how precious life is, and how fragile. How different tonight would be, I think, if Dad had not survived open-heart surgery.

His problems were discovered in May when he went to donate blood. While routinely checking his heart, the nurse found an abnormality. In a matter of weeks, his condition had deteriorated to the point where he could hardly walk across the room without feeling exhausted, even faint. Finally, he agreed to see a doctor, who immediately admitted him into the hospital.

An angiogram revealed that the main artery was 95 percent blocked, and a second artery was more than 60 percent obstructed. Bypass surgery was the only remedy. Dad wanted to postpone the operation for a few days, but the doctor wouldn't hear of it.

"Every day that you delay increases your risks of a major heart attack," he explained.

Reluctantly, Dad agreed, and surgery was scheduled for the next morning.

In the intervening hours, Dad came face to face with his own mortality. When he and I were alone, he blinked to hold back his tears as he told me all the things he wanted to do for Mother and hadn't got to, at least not yet. Foremost among them was a trip to Hawaii where he had served during the Second World War.

"We dreamed of celebrating our twenty-fifth anniversary on the islands," he told me in a voice hauntingly sad, "but we couldn't afford it. Now we may never get to go."

He must have mentioned the same thing to the other children as well, because as soon as he was out of danger we began conspiring to provide an all-expense-paid trip for the two of them. My brother Bob took care of all the details, and by Christmas the arrangements had been made. All that remained was the joy of presenting the tickets.

Finally, Don (my missionary brother who is home from Argentina) hands them their gift, and we all hold our breath as Mother removes the brightly colored bow and holiday wrapping. She gasps with excitement when she sees the pictures of Hawaii and the airline tickets, then begins to cry.

"You shouldn't have," she says. "You kids can't afford to do this."

Dad simply sits there, with a silly grin on his face, trying to pretend he isn't surprised at all. As happy as Mother and Dad are, their joy cannot compare with ours for we experience the special joy of helping make a dream come true for someone we love.

This is just one of several times that I have had the privilege of experiencing the joy of giving. Once, when I gave my wool overcoat to a homeless man on a bitterly cold December day, I thought my heart would burst, so great was my joy. That grateful man wrapped his arms around me and pulled me to his chest in a bear hug. He smelled like booze and body odor and damp clothes, but I didn't mind. His was the holiest hug I have ever received. In truth, it seemed as if God Himself were hugging me.

Then there's the Christmas I gave Brenda a special gift. For at least three years she had cherished a poem I had written titled, "Joy Is a Many-Splendored Thing." When we printed it on the cover of our church bulletin, she cut it out and, using a magnet, fastened it on our refrigerator door, where it stayed for more than two years.

Without letting her know what I was doing, I had the poem done in calligraphy, then matted and framed. When she unwraps it, on Christmas Eve, she gasps with surprise, and then tears of joy spill down her cheeks. With a tender poignancy she begins to read:

"Joy is a many-splendored thing —
a phone call from an old friend,
a good book,
a second cup of coffee,
a warm fire on a winter night.
It's life's little pleasures,
autumn colors,
the season's first snow,
the sound of rain on a tin roof,
the pungent odor of a dusty barn
resurrecting childhood memories
of haylofts and hide 'n seek."

Overcome with emotion, she stops reading. For a long while neither of us speak; we just look at each other with eyes full of love. Finally, I put my arm around her and began to read, picking up where she left off:

"...Joy is a many-splendored thing —
a strange and wonderful mixture
     of love and laughter,
          pain and sorrow,
               life and death.
It's the comfort of friends
when you stand beside the open grave
of the one you've loved and lived with
     your whole life long.
It's the strength of Scripture
     in the dark hour of unspeakable need.
It's the memory of His faithfulness,
     the promise of His presence.
Joy is a many-splendored thing."

"Richard..." The way she says my name makes my heart ache with happiness, and I smile as she says, "...this is the most wonderful gift you have ever given me. I'll always cherish it."

Special though my gift is, it cannot compare with the gift Brenda had given me two years earlier on the night of December 24, 1988. For the first time ever, we are celebrating Christmas alone. Determining to make the best of it, I build a fire in the fireplace and light the kerosine lamps on the mantle while Brenda prepares eggnog in the kitchen.

After a bit she comes to join me in front of the fire, but instead of sitting beside me on the love seat, she kneels behind me and puts both arms around my neck. "I have something for you," she says, handing me a red envelope.

A Christmas card, I think, how nice. Then I see a handwritten note beneath the printed verse. As I begin to read, my eyes grow misty, and my throat aches, so great is the lump that forms there.

In an instant I am transported back to a Sunday afternoon in August nearly ten years earlier. We are quarreling, as married couples are wont to do, as we have done numerous times before during our thirteen-year marriage. I have long since forgotten what started it, some insignificant thing most likely, but it soon turns deadly serious.

And then Brenda speaks the words that seem to seal my fate. "I can't live this way," she says, "I won't. When Leah graduates, I am going to divorce you."

We never speak of that tragic Sunday afternoon again. But for years, nine years and four months to be exact, that painful moment lies like a piece of misplaced furniture in the soul of our relationship. Any time we try to get close to each other, we bump into it.

As the years pass, things improve between us. Many a night I lie on the bed watching Brenda as she prepares to join me, and think how blessed we are. Not infrequently I ask her, "Do you think anyone is as happy as we are?" Giving me a quick smile and a hug, before turning out the light, she always says, "I'm sure there are others just as happy."

Lying in the darkness I think, "It's going to be all right. She's happier now, I can tell." But oh, how I long to hear her say, "Richard, all is forgiven. I don't hate you any more. I love you. I could never divorce you." I can't ask though, lest I awaken her old hurts. I can only wait. And hope.

In May 1988 Leah graduates from high school and leaves home to begin a life of her own. Now it is just the two of us, Brenda and me. June turns into December, and before we hardly know it, it is Christmas Eve...

I strain to make out Brenda's words through tear-blurred eyes. Haltingly I read: "I Brenda Starr take thee Richard Dean to be my lawfully wedded husband. To have and to hold from this day forward. For richer, for poorer, in sickness and in health, till death do us part. To love, honor, cherish and obey. Forsaking all others and thereto I plight thee my troth. In the name of the Father, the Son and the Holy Ghost.

"It looks like you're stuck with me! I'm not going anywhere! Always remember 'I'll never leave thee nor forsake thee.'

Your Devoted Wife & Lover,

Brenda Starr"

This is what I have yearned for since that tragic Sunday afternoon in August nearly ten years ago. This is what I have been dying to receive, but could never ask for. This is what I so desperately need, but do not deserve – Brenda's love and her forgiveness.

All at once I am undone, overwhelmed, by such mercy and grace. With tears streaming down my cheeks I turn to Brenda and crush her to my chest. The awful burden of ten long years is lifted. The dark cloud of condemnation is dissipated. That misplaced piece of furniture is gone. There is nothing between us. In the soul of our marriage there is only love, and we are one.

As we hug, I am sure I hear the angels singing as they sang that first Christmas so long ago. And in the midst of their heavenly song I hear another voice, louder than the rest. It says, "'...you are to give him the name Jesus, because he will save his people from their sins.'"[1]

He has, thank God, He has!

---

[1] Matthew 1:21.

The whole Christmas story is filled with miracles,
    like angelic visitations
    and divine dreams,
    which pale to insignificance
    in light of the really big Miracle −
        a virgin giving birth
            to the Son of God!

I cannot comprehend it,
    it makes no sense to me.
How could the infinite, eternal God
    become a tiny baby?
And not only how, but why?
Why would He choose to be born to peasant parents?
Why would He empty Himself
    of every advantage of His divine nature?
Why would He choose to become a servant
    to the race He created?
Why would He humble Himself
    and become obedient to death,
        even death on a cross?
This mystery is too great for me.
I cannot comprehend it,

I cannot explain it,
> but I accept it!

For reasons,
> which only His holy love can explain,
>> God chose to become one of us,
>> to suffer the consequences of our sin
>> in order to give birth to the miracle of forgiveness.

When I accept His holy love,
> His gift of forgiveness,
> a Christmas miracle happens in my own life.
> My sinful past,
> those selfish, hurtful acts,
> those pieces of misplaced furniture
> which separate me from those I love
>> and from God,
> are suddenly gone and we are one!

Forgiveness does not change the past,
> nothing can do that,
> but it does something better,
> it unlocks the future
> and that's the greatest miracle of all,
> the ultimate miracle of Christmas.

C H A P T E R
7

The Truth About Christmas

" *I*n truth, Christmas
is a lot like life."

Chapter 7

The Truth About Christmas

*F*or many of us, Christmas fails to live up to its billing. Instead of peace and good cheer, we contend with twenty-five-hour days, overdrafts and last-minute shopping sprees. Our nerves are rubbed raw, set on edge by traffic jams, irritated by shoppers gone mad. Even in the midst of holiday festivities, we sometimes experience a haunting loneliness and bury our silent tears beneath a wall of laughter.

Surely, we tell ourselves, Christmas is supposed to be more than this, more than empty cheer and season's greetings, born of obligation, sent without meaning. Surely Christmas is supposed to be more than just another round in our bumper-car existence:

"How are you doing?"

  bump, bump.

"Great party, isn't it!"

  bump, bump, bump...

In truth, Christmas is a lot like life. It's full of contradictions and no little confusion. It's filled with both the good and the bad, with all of the generosity and all of the greed that is so characteristic of our fallen race, with all of humanity's pride and all of its shame. And into this hodgepodge He came, was made flesh, was born a baby in a sheep shed. And nothing has been the same since, not for Mary and Joseph, nor for the shepherds, nor for the world for that matter.

Like life, Christmas is a mixture of the miraculous and the mundane. I mean, what could be more miraculous than a visit from the angel Gabriel, unless it was the message he brought: "You will be with child," he told thirteen-year-old Mary, "and give birth to a son, and you are to give him the name Jesus. He will be great and will be called the Son of the Most High...."[1]

What could be more miraculous than a virgin conceiving a child? And not just any child either, but the Son of God. Think about it. The infinite, eternal God becoming a tiny embryo in Mary's womb. There is nothing more miraculous than that.

Yet, it only took a few minutes for these miraculous events to transpire, and then life returned to the mundane. It's safe to say, I think,

---

[1]Luke 1:31,32.

that following the miracle of the Holy Spirit's visitation, the reality of Mary's situation began to dawn on her. Though still a virgin, she is pregnant. She who has never known a man is with child. Exciting? Yes, but dreadful too. How is she going to explain this to her parents? To Joseph?

And like expectant mothers in every age, she suffers the painful distress of morning sickness. Morning sickness, no less! Can you imagine that? The conception was supernatural, miraculous, but the pregnancy was not. This too is part and parcel of Christmas – the strange and wonderful blending of the miraculous and the mundane.

Like any teen-age girl who suddenly discovers she is pregnant out of wedlock, Mary sometimes feels overwhelmed. Once her condition becomes common knowledge, she is fair game for the village wags. "Have you heard about Mary?" they whisper behind the backs of their hands. "For shame. For shame." Likely it got so bad that she was forced to seek refuge with her cousin Elizabeth who lived some distance away in the hill country of Judea.[2]

Dealing with the slander of the village wags, though, is nothing compared to the trauma of telling Joseph. I can imagine Mary telling

---

[2]Luke 1:39,40.

Elizabeth, "(When) I told Joseph. He stared at me as if this were some strange tale that defied belief. Watching his face, suddenly drawn and pained, I watched the doubt overtake all the trust that once he placed in me. I told him this child was conceived by the Holy Spirit — he looked at me as if I had broken every bond between us.

"He seemed at first as if a sword had pierced his soul. And the agony on his face was so intense, there was no way that I could ease that pain or reassure him of my love.

"I watched the sorrow in his eyes change — in moments change from grief to anger. My words could not undo the path his thoughts had taken. He felt the pain that any man would feel, believing the woman he trusted and loved — the woman whose hand he had never so much as touched — could play him false.

"I wept — and he as well. Though my tears were for him, his were in anger and reproach.

"He said he would not go through with the marriage. He said he would break the promise of our families and take a bride more worthy of his trust."[3]

---

[3]Marilee Zdenek, *Someone Special* (Waco: Word Books Publisher, 1977), no page numbers.

Thankfully, while Joseph is considering these things he experiences his own Christmas miracle – "...an angel of the Lord appeared to him in a dream and said, 'Joseph son of David, do not be afraid to take Mary home as your wife, because what is conceived in her is from the Holy Spirit.'"[4]

"When Joseph woke up, he did what the angel of the Lord had commanded him and took Mary home as his wife. But he had no union with her until she gave birth to a son. And he gave him the name Jesus."[5]

Unfortunately, there is nothing miraculous about the trip to Bethlehem. Mary is nine months pregnant, huge with child and riding on the back of a donkey day after day. It is just a long, hard journey. Grueling beyond imagining, to tell the unvarnished truth. Nor is there anything miraculous about the birth either. It is messy like all births are messy, and painful as all births are painful. And to complicate matters, Mary is forced to give birth in a sheep shed out behind an inn in which there is no room for them.

Oh, there were some other miracles that first Christmas – angelic choirs, Magi from afar, another God-given dream for Joseph and a

---

[4]Matthew 1:20.
[5]Matthew 1:24,25.

miraculous escape to Egypt. But, for the most part, it was more mundane than miraculous. There was no room in the inn, taxes had to be paid and Joseph was hard-pressed to find a way to make a living for his wife and newborn son.

That's the way it is in our lives too. God is suddenly, supernaturally, present, and we are overwhelmed, undone, by His nearness. We experience a Christmas of our own, be it June or December, and we worship Him. But these epiphanies are momentary at best, and then life presses in again in all of its ordinariness.

That's the reality of Christmas, isn't it? The shepherds return to their sheep, Joseph returns to his carpenter shop and life goes on as if nothing unusual has happened. It's the same for us too. In spite of all the miracles, we still have to contend with the same stuff that everyone else contends with. The children get sick, the car breaks down, we have trouble making ends meet. Nothing major, just life's little hangnails.

Though life is the same, yet it is not exactly the same either, for now we are not alone. In the midst of our lostness and loneliness, He is suddenly there. Immanuel – God with us![6] And His presence stills our internal storms of doubt and fear. The touch of His hand makes all things

---

[6]Matthew 1:23.

new. Suddenly we know who He is, and who we are. And like the angels of old, we hear ourselves praising God and saying, "Glory to God in the highest, and on earth peace, good will toward men."[7]

Now the test comes. Will we treasure these moments? Will we hide them in our heart as Mary did?[8] Will we protect them in the same way that Joseph protected the baby Jesus from the homicidal madness of King Herod?[9] Will we keep Christmas alive in our hearts all year long? Or will we succumb to the press of busyness and let Christmas fade into a dim memory? The choice is ours. For in the end, only we can keep Christmas alive in our hearts.

---

[7]Luke 2:14 KJV.

[8]Luke 2:19.

[9]Matthew 2:13-18.